LUNCH MATTERS

THE ROLE OF THE LUNCHTIME SUPERVISOR
PLAY
BEHAVIOUR MANAGEMENT

by
DEBRA BREWER
and
HEATHER SWAIN
EDUCATIONAL PSYCHOLOGISTS

Cumbria County Psychological Service

NASEN

A NASEN Publication

Published by NASEN.
NASEN is a registered charity. Charity No. 1007023.
NASEN is a company limited by guarantee, registered in England and Wales.
Company No. 2674379.

Further copies of this book and details of NASEN's many other publications may be obtained
from the NASEN Bookshop at its registered office:
NASEN House, 4/5, Amber Business Village, Amber Close, Amington, Tamworth, Staffs., B77 4RP.
Tel: 01827 311500 Fax: 01827 313005 email: welcome@nasen.org.uk
Website: www.nasen.org.uk

Illustrations by Ian McDonald.
Cover design by Raphael Creative Design.
Typeset by J. C. Typesetting.
Typeset in Times and printed in the United Kingdom by Stowes (Stoke-on-Trent).

LUNCH MATTERS

Contents

Acknowledgements

Many people have helped in various ways in the compilation of these training materials. All are greatly appreciated. We would particularly like to express our thanks to colleagues within Cumbria County Psychological Service for their constructive support and advice. Special thanks to Ann-Marie Bunting for patient and efficient administrative support.

We also wish to recognise the valuable contributions made by lunchtime supervisors who have participated in Lunch Matters training in Cumbria.

Illustrations by Ian McDonald.

Guide to the Materials

What is Lunch Matters?

Lunch Matters is a practical training course for lunchtime supervisors working in a primary school context. It encourages supervisors to reflect on their own situation and to adopt a problem-solving approach to meeting demands and difficulties. The course is designed to run over three two-hour sessions:

Session 1: The role of the lunchtime supervisor
Session 2: The importance of play and ideas for encouraging play
Session 3: Strategies for behaviour management

After the initial training course, presenters may wish to complete follow-up work with individual schools to encourage supervisors to apply skills and knowledge within their own particular context.

Who is the training for?

Although it would be possible to organise the training within an individual school, in practice it has been helpful to have supervisors from more than one school meeting together to share information and ideas. A group of 25-30 supervisors is ideal.

We have found it useful to have *all* supervisors from a school at the training sessions to encourage a whole school approach. This also provides opportunities for mutual support when supervisors develop ideas from the training on their return to school. We therefore chose to base the cost of the course on the size of a school, rather than on the number of supervisors who would be attending, to encourage schools to send as many staff as possible.

Venue and timing

Given that supervisors may have just a short time to travel between school and the course venue, a central and convenient location would be appropriate. You will need to provide an overhead projector (OHP), screen, flipchart and tea/coffee facilities if these are not provided by the venue you have chosen. A suitable seating arrangement would be a horseshoe shape.

In practice it has proved helpful to run the course between 9.30 am and 11.30 am. This allows time for supervisors to drop off their own children at school and then to return to school for the lunchtime. A prompt finish has been appreciated.

Who can deliver the course?

It is assumed that course presenters will have knowledge and skills relating to an understanding of child development and play and issues surrounding the management of behaviour. Psychologists, specialist teachers and advisory staff may be particularly interested in offering this training.

Although it would be possible for one person to deliver the course, in our experience having two presenters has proved helpful. This offers participants alternative presentation styles and provides presenters with the support of a peer.

Successful organisation and management will depend on adapting approaches to individual circumstances. For this reason course leaders need to reflect on the experiences and difficulties supervisors bring in order to illustrate and exemplify the points being made in each session. Equally course presenters should be able to use anecdotes and humour to support the basic materials. Supervisors should be encouraged to comment and ask questions. Time constraints will demand careful management of such discussions.

Before the course

It may be helpful for schools to consider general playground issues, the status of lunchtime supervisors and some aspects of their whole school organisation before supervisors attend the course. Suggestions relating to these issues are appended and could be sent to schools or discussed with teaching staff if appropriate.

An outline of the materials

There are presentation notes for course leaders for each of the three sessions which include information on timing and necessary materials. These are supplemented through the use of OHP transparencies which are photocopiable. Cards to support activities used are also supplied. For each session it has been beneficial to produce booklets of the OHPs for the course participants to refer to.

An agenda and an example of a certificate to present to supervisors at the end of the course are included in the appendix.

Additional reading

Suggestions for additional reading are appended (see page 87).

Play and Lunchtimes in the Primary School

All school children, school staff and other adults will have experiences and memories of the playground. These may be positive, with play and lunchtimes perceived as opportunities to socialise, to let off steam, to play and to rest. Equally, though, pupils and school staff may, at some time, find play and lunchtimes cause anxiety and give rise to concerns over the nature of play, behaviour and socialisation experienced and observed in and around the playground.

Time and Space

We must not lose sight of the fact that play and lunchtimes form a significant part of the school day, taking up to 21% of the day at the junior stage and up to 24% for infants (Blatchford, 1998).

The playground itself also takes up a significant proportion of the school grounds. Thus, at school, playtimes feature heavily in terms of time and space.

Play and Lunchtimes as Learning Opportunities

Given that the school grounds can take up so much space, there is increasing interest in using this as a learning environment. Projects have involved the delivery of aspects of the National Curriculum, developing nature reserves, expanding children's environmental awareness and involving children in the design of playgrounds. Some schools have taken steps to improve the playground through creative markings, having large and small play equipment and sectioning the grounds. Measures such as these expand the opportunities for play.

Additionally playtimes have been a focus for the involvement of children in conflict resolution through circle time and children's councils.

Playground Games

It has long been recognised that play is important in children's development. There has also been observation and reporting on the nature of children's play. The Opies (1969) described a colourful portrayal of children's play involving marbles, clapping, chasing, catching, seeking, guessing games, skipping, acting, singing and rhyming.

More recent observations (Blatchford, 1989) indicate some decline in these traditional games, particularly so in dialogue games. Movement games, such as football and feats of physical prowess, appear to be as prevalent, if not more so. Speculation has arisen as to the impact on children's language and literacy development with this decline in rhyming, singing and talking games.

The Purpose of Play and Lunchtimes

Aside from using the school grounds and observations of the nature of children's play, there has been some debate as to the actual purpose of playtimes. By the very existence of a break, staff and children are provided with an opportunity to use the toilet, seek refreshment and have a break from work. It is argued also that children can 'let off steam' by running around the playground, chatting and playing with friends.

However, it is also argued that there is more to play and lunchtimes than opportunities for a work break. Slukin (1981) and Grudgeon (1993) both suggest the most important aims of play and lunchtimes relate to opportunities for social interaction. It is at play and lunchtimes that children are able to learn skills for adult life, such as cooperating, taking turns, forming attitudes and understanding rules.

Such skills may of course be learned and practiced in other situations, but play and lunchtimes offer a unique context. Supervision is limited, rules and structure differ from other contexts, such as the classroom, and children are leading the activities and play. Some studies suggest that play and lunchtimes have a different culture to that of the classroom. Sutton-Smith (1990) describes play and lunchtimes as a time to engage in activities with their own rules, language, boundaries, gestures and traditions.

Further, the significance of the socialisation opportunities created by play and lunchtimes has grown over time with the decline of play outside of school. Increasingly there are fewer opportunities for children of primary school age to interact freely with peers away from school (Hillman, 1993).

Research into Play and Lunchtimes

Having established that play and lunchtimes take a great deal of time and space and are vital to the development of children's socialisation, since the late 1980s research has been gathering some momentum.

From this research a worrying picture has emerged concerning:

- the limited use made of the school grounds;
- children's behaviour in the playground;
- aggression;
- the amount of desultory behaviours;
- a decline in traditional games;
- discrimination against some children;
- management and supervision issues pertinent to play and lunchtimes.

Within the teaching profession, the media and local communities a similarly worrying perception has developed in relation to children's socialisation and behaviour at school generally and during play and lunchtimes more specifically. In 1989 the Elton committee of 'Enquiry into Discipline in Schools' (DES, 1989) identified the lunch break as 'the single biggest behaviour related problem that (staff) face'.

The Perceptions and Experiences of Teachers and Children

Teaching staff are reported to find that play and lunchtimes can set the tone for subsequent lessons. Children who have found the playtime stressful in some way find it difficult to concentrate on their work. Their self-esteem may be adversely affected. Loud and uncontrolled playtime behaviour may be continued once in the classroom. Grievances which stem from the playground may be carried into the classroom and even taken home.

Interviews with children have indicated that whilst many have a positive view of play and lunchtimes there are some aspects which they do not like. Blatchford (1998) identified that children were aware of and worried about disruptive behaviours (bullying, fighting), having nothing to do, the threat of physical or verbal aggression, and frustrations arising from games (eg space being limited). The weather was also identified as a less positive aspect of play and lunchtimes.

More specifically Whitney and Smith (1993) reported that most bullying appears to take place on school playgrounds. Concerns have also developed over racist name calling (Kelly, 1988) and teasing (Mooney, Creeser & Blatchford, 1991). Difficulties for younger children and quiet children have been observed, often with such children on the periphery of games, with limited opportunity and space to engage in play of their own choosing. Differences in the play and attitudes between boys and girls has evoked some interest (Thorne, 1993; Blatchford, 1998). Girls seem to be less positive about playtimes and more inclined to worry. The nature of play between the two can vary also, especially as they get older (Kelly, 1994; Blatchford, 1998).

As Kelly (1994) stresses, these studies and others like them highlight the issues of 'equal opportunities', the experiences some children have at playtimes and how children learn to deal with matters of injustice and inequality.

Summary

Play and lunchtimes are a significant feature of school life. The grounds are a useful resource and opportunities for play are invaluable in children's learning and development. The process of play and experiences in the playground contributes towards the development of social skills which may be adopted in adult life.

This notwithstanding, the experiences of children and school staff detail problems which stem from play and lunchtimes. There is a growing body of research which identifies a range of difficulties relating to changes in play, inequality, behaviour and management issues at play and lunchtimes. These difficulties are said to have some influence on how children can settle to work in class, on their self-esteem, their behaviour and socialisation more generally and opportunities for learning.

Therefore, proactive intervention to improve children's experiences of play and lunchtimes is vital.

The Training of Lunchtime Supervisors

In 1989, the Elton Report 'Discipline in Schools' recommended that:

'LEAs and governing bodies which employ school staff should ensure that midday supervisors are given training in the management of pupil behaviour'. (DES, 1989, 131.1)

The report recognised that lunchtime is a vital and often neglected aspect of school life and that, as suggested previously, behaviour at lunchtimes could have significant effects on classroom behaviour and learning.

Following the Elton Report several local authorities developed their own training materials. Details of some of these earlier courses are included in the appendix of further reading. The present course attempts to make training materials for lunchtime supervisors much more widely available to all schools. Lunch Matters has been extensively trialled and developed in Cumbria to provide practical, easy-to-use materials which could be used to provide initial training to lunchtime supervisors working in any primary setting.

The Benefits of Training Lunchtime Supervisors

Sharp (1994) reports that some of the key benefits of training lunchtime supervisors are:

- improved communications between teaching staff and supervisors;
- greater self-confidence amongst supervisors;
- reduced referral of problems to headteacher/teacher;
- more respect for supervisors from teachers, pupils and parents;
- more constructive handling of difficult situations;
- de-escalation of conflict;
- more orderly lunchtimes, more positive atmosphere;
- happier children.

Within Cumbria, similar reports have been received from supervisors who have attended Lunch Matters training courses over the past five years.

The Importance of a Whole School Approach

Although the training of lunchtime supervisors is seen as a key element in promoting more positive lunchtimes, there is agreement in the research literature that to be maximally effective, the training needs to be part of a co-ordinated whole school approach (eg Sharp, 1994; White & Wilkinson, 1996). Such an approach would involve children, parents, school staff, governors and the wider community. By planning and working together to increase opportunities at lunchtimes and to decrease inappropriate behaviours and activities, the effectiveness of the training of lunchtime supervisory staff is enhanced. The Elton Report (DES, 1989) suggested that lunchtime supervisors should be involved in decision making and policy development and should be seen as valued and important members of the school community.

As part of such a whole school approach to lunchtimes it may be helpful to consider:

- issues of whole school organisation and how these will be reviewed and evaluated. For example, the length of lunchtimes, the roles and responsibilities of staff on duty and the way in which children are grouped and moved may all need attention;
- improving the status of lunchtime supervisors and improving opportunities for communication between supervisors and others working within the school;
- what environmental changes might be needed to promote play and to minimise the risk of disruption;
- whether there are wider in-service and training implications for the school. For example, joint training in behaviour management/social skills/peer relationships may be considered appropriate for all staff, including lunchtime supervisors.

Within the materials there are further suggestions regarding areas that a school may wish to consider before using the training pack with supervisors. These are suggestions only and should not take the place of a careful and constructive evaluation of the unique circumstances that each individual school may present.

Aims of Lunch Matters

- To provide opportunities for lunchtime supervisors to explore their own opinions and attitudes towards lunchtime issues.
- To develop lunchtime supervisors' skills and confidence in:
  (i)   planning and organising lunchtimes;
  (ii) promoting and developing play;
  (iii) managing behaviour.
- To develop lunchtime supervisors' knowledge and understanding of child development more generally and the impact of playground experiences.
- To promote a problem-solving approach to the management of lunchtime issues.
- To encourage a whole school approach to the development of lunchtimes, where lunchtime supervisors are seen as an essential and integral part of a staff team.

LUNCH MATTERS

Session 1
The Role of the
Lunchtime Supervisor

Presentation Notes

Session 1
The Role of the Lunchtime Supervisor

Overview and Aims

This first session provides opportunities for lunchtime supervisors to begin to work with colleagues from other schools. Initial activities encourage participation and aim to develop supervisors' confidence in sharing experiences, opinions and ideas.

Emphasis is placed on exploring and reflecting on their role and on their personal qualities and skills. Issues of organisation and planning are introduced and the importance of a whole school approach is highlighted.

Underpinning such discussions and activities is a problem-solving approach.

On their return to school, supervisors are encouraged to have initial discussions with teaching staff over issues identified by this session, for example, any concerns they might have about their role.

Presentation Notes

Before Session 1

- Photocopy a set of OHP transparencies (pages 20-26) for each course participant.
- Photocopy Activity Card B 'Aspects of My Role in School (page 28) - one for each participant.
- Photocopy Activity Sheet C 'Agreeing Rules' (page 29) - one copy per two participants.
- Photocopy Activity D Cards 'Tricky Situations' (page 30) - a different situation for each group of four to five supervisors.
- Photocopy Activity D Response Sheets (page 31) - one per course participant.
- Assign course participants to groups of four to five supervisors, ensuring that each group contains a mix of supervisors from different schools.
- Prepare Registration Sheet for participants to sign.
- Collect together books and resources concerning playtimes/lunchtimes for display during the session.

Materials needed during the session

- OHP
- Flipchart Paper
- Pens

Introduction

Welcome supervisors to the course. Outline the programme for the three sessions. Emphasise that comments and questions are welcome and are a valuable part of the course. Suggest that the overall aims of the course are to encourage them to share ideas and experiences and to develop the skills needed to promote successful lunchtimes in their own schools.

Give details of the agenda for this first session which aims to explore the role and skills of the lunchtime supervisor and how to plan effectively for lunchtimes.

Indicate that a booklet containing copies of OHP transparencies will be available at the end of the session.

5 mins

Lunchtime in the School Day

OHP 1 (see page 20)

Ask supervisors to guess what percentage of the school day children spend having breaktime. Emphasise that this is a significant part of their time in school. Contrast these figures with those relating to time spent on other curriculum areas (eg Tizard, Blatchford, Burke, Farquhar and Plewis, 1988, suggested this could be as little as reading 2%, writing 9%, maths 8%). Also draw attention to the amount of space which the playground usually occupies and the potential of this space for providing learning opportunities for children.

Discuss the relatively limited research available relating to lunchtimes and the relative lack of training available for staff. Draw supervisors' attention to any resources/materials which you may have brought with you. (Ideas for these are included in the appendices.)

25 mins

The Role of the Lunchtime Supervisor

Activity A

Ask supervisors working in their assigned groups to list on a piece of flipchart paper *all* jobs which they do during the lunch period. Encourage discussion of similarities and differences.

As a whole group comment on the range of jobs they undertake and discuss areas where training might be helpful. Stress the importance of their role in promoting children's play and social development.

Activity B (see page 28)

Ask supervisors working individually to complete ***Activity Card B*** regarding their own perception of their role. Suggest that on their return to school they discuss these points with other supervisors and staff. Indicate that the outcome of these discussions will be considered at the beginning of the next session.

Relationships with Children and Staff

10-15 mins

OHP 2 (see page 21)

Highlight that regardless of their role, supervisors need to possess certain personal qualities and skills. Of particular importance is their ability to relate to children and staff.

Working with the whole group, ask supervisors to respond to the points on ***OHP 2***. Encourage general discussion rather than suggesting that any one answer is necessarily correct.

Often the issues of giving orders and shouting at children are of particular concern to supervisors. Talk through ***OHP 3*** (see page 22) giving examples as appropriate and encouraging comments from supervisors.

Break

Break for tea, coffee and biscuits.

15 mins

Organisation and Planning

15 mins

Highlight that regardless of their personal qualities and skills, supervisors will also need to consider organisation and planning.

OHP 4 (see page 23)

Talk through the OHP giving appropriate examples. Encourage supervisors to talk about practice in their own school.

OHP 5 (see page 24)

One feature of a school's organisation would be the effective communication of positive rules. Talk through the OHP giving examples where necessary.

Activity C (see page 29)
OHP 6 (see page 25)

Ask supervisors working in pairs to rewrite the statements on the ***Activity C sheet*** (see page 29) to be as positive and specific as possible. Take feedback and discuss.

15 mins

25 mins

Tricky Situations

The aim of the 'tricky situations' is to encourage supervisors to apply and consolidate the information they have considered during this first session.

OHP 7 (see page 26)
Present the 'tricky situation' to the whole group. Invite discussion on what immediate action supervisors would take and on how they would plan for the future. In particular encourage supervisors to examine the organisation of lunchtimes (eg improving liaison between teachers and supervisors, ensuring that areas are not left unsupervised for lengthy periods).

Activity D (see pages 30 and 31)
Working in their previously assigned groups, supervisors should discuss and record on the *Activity D Card* their responses to the 'tricky situation' which their group has been allocated.

Take feedback highlighting pertinent points relating to the issues discussed during the session.

LUNCH MATTERS

Session 1
The Role of the
Lunchtime Supervisor

OHP Transparencies

DURATION OF BREAKTIME

	Minutes	% of school day
Infant (5-7 years)	93	24%
Junior (7-11 years)	83	21%

Blatchford (1998)

RELATIONSHIPS WITH CHILDREN AND STAFF

Yes   Possibly   No

Smile at the children

Take the initiative in starting conversations
with children

Let children hold your hand

Get to know as many names as possible

Lose your temper with children

Talk to children about their teachers and
school work

Talk to children about their family

Tell children off in front of their friends

Answer personal questions you are asked

Discuss tricky situations with other supervisors

ORDERS AND SHOUTING

Orders
Should only be used when necessary because they can lead to confrontation.

Shouting
Should only be used when necessary because it can be stressful and cause resentment.

'Oh dear!'
'I wonder if she's cross with me?'

ORGANISATION AND PLANNING

- Needs to be a whole school plan - including teachers, children and parents.

- What are the rules and routines?

- What happens during wet lunchtimes?

- What rewards and sanctions are available?

- How is liaison with teachers organised?

- What happens in the event of emergencies?

- Are there any children with special needs you need to be aware of?

RULES OF THE PLAYGROUND

Agree the rules of the playground *with* the children, staff and parents. Everybody then knows how they ought to behave.

- Phrase them clearly so they are easy for children to understand.
- Spend time discussing the rules.
- Avoid a list of 'Do nots'.
- Display the rules in school.
- Keep the list short.

Agree *with* the children, staff and parents how you will deal with the children who don't follow these rules. This ensures that:

- everybody deals with unwanted behaviour in the same way;
- the children know the consequences of not following the rules.

For instance, you might agree that a child who has written on wall will always be expected to clean the wall, or it might be agreed that a child who is running wildly about the playground will always miss some playtime.

AGREEING RULES

1. Don't run down the corridor

2. Not too many children in the toilet at one time

3. We don't kick each other

You have noticed that Susan has been in the cloakroom crying for most of the lunchtime.

Session 1: OHP 7

LUNCH MATTERS

Session 1
The Role of the
Lunchtime Supervisor

Activity Materials

ASPECTS OF MY ROLE IN SCHOOL

An area I have concerns about…

An area which I could develop…

AGREEING RULES

1. Don't run down the corridor

2. Not too many children in the toilet at one time

3. We don't kick each other

TRICKY SITUATIONS

- Year 2 often come out of class early for lunch and line up by the technology display.

- The children often go onto the field and get muddy. They say Mr Brown told them they could.

- A man comes into the playground and starts talking to a group of young children.

- You have noticed that Susan has been in the cloakroom for most of the lunchtime.

- A group of children are just leaving the dining hall and you notice that their table is messy and water has been spilt on the floor.

- Wayne never seems to join in games with the other children.

- A parent comes into the playground complaining that John's anorak was torn and dirty after school yesterday. She says this happened during lunchtime.

- After a wet lunchtime the classteacher complained to the supervisor that new marker pens from the cupboard had been used and no longer had any lids.

- Gail never seems to listen or follow instructions. You are beginning to wonder if her hearing is alright.

Session 1: Activity D

TRICKY SITUATIONS

Immediate Action

Future Planning

LUNCH MATTERS

Session 2
Play

Presentation Notes

Session 2
Play

Overview and Aims

The session on play aims to develop supervisors' understanding of what play is and how it is important to a child's development.

Building on the work introduced in the first session, ideas for developing play are discussed within a whole school framework for organisation and planning.

Working collaboratively, supervisors are encouraged to explore solutions to potential difficulties which arise from particular games, playground equipment and weather conditions.

Issues relating to equality of opportunity for children are addressed.

Presentation Notes

Before Session 2

- Photocopy a set of OHP transparencies (pages 40-46) for each course participant.
- Photocopy Activity B record sheets (page 48) - one per group.
- Collect equipment for Activity C (listed in the presentation notes). (See page 38).
- Photocopy Activity C Cards 'Equipment Game' (page 49) - four per group.
- Photocopy Activity E Cards 'Three Tips for Wet Lunchtimes' (page 50) - one per course participant.
- Prepare Registration Sheet for participants to sign.

Materials needed during the session

- OHP
- Flipchart Paper
- Pens
- Equipment (listed for Activity C)

Introduction

Welcome supervisors to the second session. Remind them of the agenda for the morning and re-emphasise that comments and questions are welcome. Indicate that a booklet containing copies of the OHP transparencies will be available at the end of the session.

Take feedback concerning any home assignments which were set in the previous session on organisation and planning.

Ask more generally if supervisors have had an opportunity to discuss the course with teaching staff.

Why Have a Playtime?

5 mins

OHP 1 (see page 40)
Use the OHP to explain why children/teachers need a playtime. Emphasise the research of Andy Sluckin (1981) which highlights the importance of playtimes as an opportunity for socialisation and the importance of play in a child's development more generally.

You may wish to mention the work of Tizard et al. (1988) which suggests that very often the socialisation which children are aware of is negative in nature (eg fighting, teasing, bullying). The need for supervisors and teachers to work together to address these issues and to promote more positive social interactions should be emphasised.

What Is Play?

10 mins

Activity A
Ask supervisors to call out the games which they see children playing. Record these on the flipchart.

Supervisors will often comment on which games are played most often (eg football), difficulties which certain games precipitate (eg pretend fighting games) and contrast games which are played now with games which were played when they were younger. Questioning may begin to highlight areas of common concern which may need to be addressed later in the session. For example, supervisors may notice that football dominates available space in the playground leaving little room for other games, or that there are fewer singing and dialogue-based games than when they were younger. The difficulties which girls and quieter children meet may also be commented on.

10 mins

OHP 2 (see page 41)

Read out the definitions of play, emphasising terms relating to play being active, children having control of the play and making choices. Emphasise that play is fun, but that it is also important to a child's development and learning.

Draw supervisors' attention to the incongruencies between these definitions, some of the games they have listed previously and the difficulties they have highlighted. For example, the dominance of football or older, more boisterous children may mean that others are unable to make choices about which games they play, a lack of equipment may restrict children's choices, or a large plain expanse of tarmac may not inspire creative thought. Children may also experience pressure to conform to playing certain games at which they are not skilled and which actually promote a fear of failure.

Skills Children Learn from Play

5 mins

OHP 3 (see page 42)

Talk through the OHP, linking each skill area in turn to some examples from the list of games which the supervisors provided.

5 mins

OHP 4 (see page 43)

Select one game from the list provided by the supervisors. Emphasise that relaxation and enjoyment should be the basis of a game. In addition ask supervisors to call out any physical, language, cognitive and social skills which the game might encourage and record these on the OHP.

10 mins

Activity B (see page 48)

Ask supervisors to move into their assigned groups (from session 1). Select one or two games from the list on the flipchart and discuss and record on the ***Activity B record sheets*** the skills each game might encourage. Ask a few groups to give feedback regarding their selected games to check their understanding.

Type/Name of Game: Group Dancing		Type/Name of Game: Hopscotch	
RELAXATION AND ENJOYMENT		**RELAXATION AND ENJOYMENT**	
Physical Skills	*Language Skills*	*Physical Skills*	*Language Skills*
Coordination	Singing	Balance	Negotiating
Balance	Learning words	Throwing	Debating
Stamina	Negotiating	Drawing	Arguing
Fitness	Describing	Hopping	
	Rhythm		
Cognitive Skills	*Social Skills*	*Cognitive Skills*	*Social Skills*
Memory	Working together	Counting	Turn-taking
Left/right	Taking turns		Sharing
Rhyming	Confidence		

Break
Tea, coffee and biscuits.

15 mins

Developing Play

5 mins

OHP 5 (see page 44)
Talk through the points on the OHP giving examples to illustrate each one as necessary. Give time for supervisors to raise any queries or concerns.

You may find it helpful to refer back to the session on ***organisation and planning*** as many of the suggestions need a coordinated approach to implement effectively. For example, a system for booking in and out equipment may be useful and discussions between staff and pupils may need to take place about what play materials would be appropriate. It might also be helpful to compare the potential benefits of providing equipment against the minimal costs which could be incurred if equipment were to be lost or broken. Some discussion might also be necessary on the need for an agreed set of rules for a quiet area (eg to prevent children running in and out of school).

5 mins

OHP 6 (see page 45)
Talk through OHP. Remind supervisors of the definitions of play as being spontaneous and active and under the control of the player.

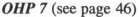

OHP 7 (see page 46)
Talk through OHP giving examples to illustrate where appropriate.

20-25 mins

Equipment Game
Activity C (see page 49)
The previously assigned groups are each allocated one piece of equipment. Supervisors are asked to devise two games for older children and two games for younger children using that equipment. Responses are recorded on the ***Equipment Game Card C***. Collect cards when they are completed. These could then be collated into a booklet to send to all participants involved in the training.

Equipment needed:
Ball, skipping rope, hoop, bean bag, chalk, pen and paper and bat and ball.

15 mins

Wet Playtime

Activity D
Brainstorm as a whole group problems which occur at wet playtimes. Record on the flipchart.

Emphasise that wet lunchtimes can be confusing for children. They may be in a classroom where they are used to working and following certain rules, but are aware that it is playtime when a different set of rules and activities apply. Clear expectations need to be established.

It might be useful to use some of the points raised to highlight issues regarding the importance of organisation and planning specifically for wet lunchtimes.

Activity E (see page 50)
(This can be done either at the end of the session or as a home assignment.)

Supervisors are asked to record individually their three tips for wet lunchtimes. These might relate to the problems identified by the previous activity or might be strategies which have already been successfully implemented in their school. Responses to be recorded on the ***Activity E card***.

Following discussion and feedback, the completed cards could then be collated into the booklet to send to participants after the course.

LUNCH MATTERS

Session 2
Play

OHP Transparencies

Socialise

Law   **Fresh air**

**A break
for the
class
teacher**

PLAYTIME

**Let off
steam**

**Use the
toilet, get
a drink,
have lunch**

**To prepare
for the
next
lesson**

**Play is important
in child's development**

'Play behaviours are flexible, creative, voluntary and pleasurable. They must be self-motivated and focus on means rather than ends and are at times abstract.'

(Christie, 1991)

* * * * *

'Play is a positive and pleasureable experience for the child... Play facilitates the learning process... Play gratifies the child, fulfilling his/her emotional needs... Through play the child interacts with the environment including people and objects... Play offers an opportunity for the child to apply his/her existing thoughts and extend his/her thinking skills... Play allows the child to develop skills and knowledge for later life.'

(Sayeed and Guerin, 2000)

SKILLS CHILDREN LEARN FROM PLAY

Physical Skills   -   balance, throwing, hopping, climbing, cycling, threading, cutting, colouring

Social Skills   -   sharing, turn-taking, cooperating, leadership, caring, role play

Cognitive Skills   -   colours, counting, rhymes, sorting, matching, ordering, time

Language Skills   -   describing, negotiating, explaining, arguing, planning, listening

Type/Name of Game: ....

RELAXATION AND ENJOYMENT	
Physical Skills	***Language Skills***
Cognitive Skills	***Social Skills***

DEVELOPING PLAY

Adults can help to promote play by:

• providing playground markings and devising new ways of using them;

• encouraging children to demonstrate games to each other;

• providing equipment;

• setting aside quiet areas or other zones in the playground;

• teaching traditional games;

• organising special events/competitions;

• having a whole school approach.

ADULTS AND PLAY

'In the long run nothing extinguishes self-organised play more effectively than does action to promote it.'

(Iona and Peter Opie, 1969)

* * * * *

- Remember to involve children in planning their own play.

- Adult involvement should be about suggesting and initiating play, not taking over the game.

- Once a game is established, step in to solve problems only if children can't deal with the situation themselves.

PLAYING GAMES

- Wear suitable clothing.

- Select a suitable place to play.

- Make sure you know the rules.

- Be prepared to join in.

- Suggest games within the children's competence.

- Teach complicated games in stages.

- Try to involve everybody in some way.

- Don't persevere with games which cause problems.

- Make sure you've got all the equipment you need.

LUNCH MATTERS

Session 2
Play

Activity Materials

Type/Name of Game: ....

RELAXATION AND ENJOYMENT

Physical Skills	*Language Skills*
Cognitive Skills	*Social Skills*

EQUIPMENT GAME

Name of game:

Number of players:

Equipment needed:

Rules of game

THREE TIPS FOR WET LUNCHTIMES

1.

2.

3.

LUNCH MATTERS

Session 3
Behaviour Management

Presentation Notes

Session 3
Behaviour Management

Overview and Aims

The final session highlights that underpinning effective behaviour management there needs to be a foundation of a whole school approach. This would include clarity about roles and responsibilities, careful organisation and planning, and considered opportunities for play.

Emphasis is again placed on a collaborative, problem-solving approach to identifying and managing children's behaviour.

Within the above framework a range of possible management strategies are introduced and considered.

Issues relating to adult expectations and attitudes towards children's behavioural development are raised.

Presentation Notes

Before Session 3

- Photocopy a set of OHP transparencies (pages 60-74) for each course participant.
- Photocopy Activity A Card 'A List of Unwanted Behaviours' (page 76) - one copy per two participants.
- Photocopy Activity B Response Sheets 'Fuzzy or Non-Fuzzy?' (page 77) - one copy per two participants.
- Photocopy Activity C Cards 'Change the Setting' (page 78) - one copy per two participants.
- Photocopy Activity D Cards (page 79) - a different behavioural description per group.
- Photocopy Activity D Response Sheets 'Behaviours' (page 80).
- Prepare Registration Sheet for participants to sign.
- Prepare certificates for each participant.

Materials needed during the session

- OHP
- Flipchart Paper
- Pens

Introduction

Welcome supervisors to the third session. Remind them of the agenda and re-emphasise that comments and questions are welcome. Indicate that a booklet containing copies of OHP transparencies will be available at the end of the session.

Take feedback concerning any home assignments which were set in the previous session on play.

Ask more generally if supervisors have had an opportunity to discuss the course with teaching staff.

Emphasise that this session is working towards increased understanding of children's behaviour and the management of that behaviour. Suggest that many ideas may be familiar to supervisors but that reminders of a range of management strategies and the need for consistency between supervisors are important.

10 mins

What Are Unwanted Behaviours?

Activity A (see page 76)
Ask supervisors working in pairs to list the behaviours which they observe at lunchtimes as being difficult or unwanted. Responses can be recorded on *Activity Card A*.

OHP 1 (see page 60)
Take feedback from the groups regarding unwanted behaviours, list on OHP and add others if necessary.

Make the point that all the behaviours listed are normal and that many children will exhibit these behaviours at some point. Concerns may arise if the frequency or duration of the behaviours is higher than usual. Suggest that adults can encourage difficult behaviours through being inconsistent. Children can become confused about what is expected of them. Make sure that other problems are not contributing to difficult behaviour (eg hearing difficulties, family circumstances, speech and language difficulties, the child's stage of development). Be sensitive to the fact that children are individuals and that expectations need to be different at different ages.

5 mins

Specify the Behaviour

OHP 2 (see page 61)
Cover up the bottom half of *OHP 2*. Explain that we often describe children's behaviour using words/phrases of the type at the top of *OHP 2*. These communicate that there is a problem but do not specify clearly what that problem

is. They are 'fuzzy' descriptions of behaviour. Refer back to the list which supervisors generated on *OHP 1* to give some examples of slightly less 'fuzzy' descriptions of behaviour.

Uncover the bottom half of *OHP 2*. Explain that to deal effectively with behaviour problems we need to be less 'fuzzy' and ask questions such as those given on the OHP. Give examples to clarify this. Suggest the *'hey miss, come and watch me'* test as a way of determining whether behaviours are observable and are clearly and unambiguously described.

10 mins

OHP 3 - Activity B (see pages 62 and 77)

Working in pairs supervisors are asked to indicate which of the statements on *OHP 3* are 'fuzzy' and which are 'non-fuzzy'. It may be helpful to work through one or two examples to further explain this task. Supervisors should work in pairs and record their responses on *worksheet B*.

Take feedback from the group as a whole, explaining that some of the statements may be less 'fuzzy' than others. Additionally supervisors could be asked to think of ways in which the statements could be made less 'fuzzy'.

5-10 mins

General Behaviour Management

Write general strategies relating to behaviour management which were discussed in *session 1* on the flipchart, ie:

- the need for organisation and planning;
- the need for a whole school approach;
- the need to establish clear rules, rewards and sanctions.

Remind supervisors of the above and stress that these will underpin any other strategies they may use.

OHP 4 (see page 63)

For use on a day-to-day basis one of the most effective strategies which supervisors can use is to catch the child being good. Talk through the OHP. Suggest that supervisors may be interested to count the number of positive and negative things they say to children in a 10 minute period.

Other Possible Strategies

OHP 5 (see page 64)

Explain that ignoring is the opposite of giving attention for good behaviour. Acknowledge that this can sometimes be difficult and is not always appropriate for all behaviours/children.

OHP 6 (see page 65)

Suggest that time out is a form of planned ignoring which occurs in a set place for a specified period of time. Explain that it is effective because it removes attention and offers a consistent approach to certain behaviours. Acknowledge that it is not always effective for all children/behaviours. Some children may find it difficult to understand or be resistant to it. Emphasise the need to discuss using this strategy with children and other staff to explain how it will work when it is introduced.

OHP 7 (see page 66)

Explain that to give warnings effectively supervisors need to bear in mind the points on the OHP.

Suggest to supervisors that they might continue to observe the child and if their behaviour improves to praise them as suggested in *'catch the child being good'*.

It may be helpful to ask supervisors to give an example of how they would give warnings in a particular situation (eg a child running out of bounds).

Indicate that warnings will only be effective if supervisors keep to their word.

OHP 8 (see page 67)

The strategy of distraction can be very effective in preventing difficulties arising, but supervisors need to be very alert. Make sure that attention is not given for those behaviours which are inappropriate.

Break

Break for tea, coffee and biscuits.

10 mins

OHP 9 (see page 68)
Talk through the points on the OHP.

Activity C (see page 78)
Ask supervisors to work in pairs to discuss how they might change the setting to make the behaviours described on *OHP 9* less likely to occur. Supervisors should record their responses on *Activity Card C*. Take feedback and discuss.

10 mins

OHP 10 (see page 69)
Removing the child from the situation allows staff and children to calm down and to respond in a considered way.

OHP 11 (see page 70)
Talk through the points on the OHP, but advise supervisors to look out for those children who may be using *'making amends'* as a way of gaining attention.

OHP 12 (see page 71)
Highlight to supervisors that reasoning in a warm and non-threatening way should run through all of the suggested strategies.

5 mins

Which strategy to use?

OHP 13 (see page 72)
Emphasise the need to work through a hierarchy of strategies (thereby always giving alternative options). Such a hierarchy need not be as written on the OHP and the nature of the behaviour or the individual child may demand a different entry into the hierarchy. Give some examples.

15 mins

Activity D (see pages 79 and 80)
Ask supervisors working in their groups to discuss the behaviour outlined on the *Activity D behaviour card* allocated to them. They need to agree on:

1. what issues they would need to consider (eg home circumstances, learning difficulty);
2. how the description could be changed to a non-fuzzy (eg what further information would they need to gather);
3. what intervention they might try.

Write the above points on a flipchart as a reminder.

Put up *OHP 14* (see page 73) as a reminder of some possible strategies.

Discussions can be recorded on the *Activity D response sheet*.

Groups could be invited to provide feedback.

5 mins

Summary

Talk through *OHP 15* (see page 74) to highlight some of the main points raised during the session.

5 mins

Finally, thank them for attending. Emphasise the need to reflect on the course, discuss with colleagues and with school staff. They will need to develop an action plan in collaboration with all school staff to implement many of the issues raised during the course.

Remind them they will receive an information pack of games and wet play tips in due course.

Issue certificates.

LUNCH MATTERS

Session 3
Behaviour Management

OHP Transparencies

A LIST OF UNWANTED BEHAVIOURS

DESCRIBING BEHAVIOUR

'He's a horror'

'His behaviour... well!'

'Disruptive'

'Aggressive'

'Naughty'

But...

Who with?

What is he doing?

When does it take place?

Where does it happen?

How often?

**REMEMBER: DESCRIBE WHAT YOU SEE
HEY MISS... COME AND SEE ME...**

FUZZY OR NON-FUZZY?

Spot the fuzzy:
(Remember: is the verb observable and will the statement make sense if preceded by 'Hey miss, come and watch me...'?)

1. John likes a lot of attention from me.

2. Mark is always trying to get back into school to use the toilet.

3. Samiha sits quietly to eat her dinner.

4. Jane is always telling tales.

5. Vanessa's home situation gives considerable cause for anxiety.

6. When at the dinner table, Peter throws food into the faces of other children.

7. June gouges the table with a knife.

8. Sita likes to get the other children into trouble.

9. Bill is hyperactive.

10. Anneka pulls hair when she cannot have a toy she wants.

11. Abdullah is always rude to me.

12. Whilst waiting in the queue for his dinner, Paul pushes the children in front of him.

CATCH GOOD BEHAVIOUR AND REWARD IT

Children like attention - give it to them for the right reasons.

- If they are playing nicely, praise them.

- If they are making an effort to improve their behaviour, praise them.

'Well Jason, I'm pleased to see that you've only damaged three tables this week instead of six. Well done, it's good to see that you're making an effort.'

IGNORING

Sometimes children do things to gain attention. Simply ignoring, walking way, turning your back, whatever you feel like, but not commenting or responding in any way, is an ideal way of dealing with some behaviours.

Ignoring might be helpful for petty name calling, tale telling or some bad language.

TIME OUT

This involves removing the child from the opportunity to talk and play with others.

To use this effectively:

- everybody should know what time out is used for, how it works and where it happens;

- decide on where the child is to go, for example, standing beside the supervisor or standing in an isolated area of the playground;

- the child should only be placed in time out for 2-5 minutes;

- don't talk to the child during time out - they should be completely ignored.

It is useful to have a 'time out signal' which everybody knows so that a child can be placed in time out without being spoken to. For example, call the child's name and point to the time out area.

GIVE WARNINGS

Rather than jump down a child's throat the first time you see an unwanted behaviour, give them a warning. To do this effectively:

- make sure you have the child's attention;

- talk to them in a quiet place;

- remind them of the rule;

- say what they were doing;

- remind them of the consequences;

- suggest alternative activities;

- make sure you keep to your word.

Warnings may be helpful for children who are running around wildly, out of bounds or using bad language.

DISTRACTION

Sometimes you could anticipate unwanted behaviour or intervene swiftly once it has occurred.

You could distract a child by:

- talking to them ('That's a nice coat you've got on');

- giving them something to do ('Could you take a message for me?').

Distraction might help to prevent: spoiling others' games; fighting; telling tales; vandalism; going out of bounds.

CHANGE THE SETTING

If children always seem to behave badly in certain places, try to organise and plan to make this less likely to happen.

For example, if trouble occurs in the toilets, only allow a certain number in at once; if children seem to get restless when queuing, reduce the number allowed to queue at one time.

How could you change the setting to makc the following behaviours less likely?

1. Several children in the playground always fight to play football.

2. Chairs are knocked and pushed over as children rush to get out of the dining hall.

3. When they go around the corner to the cloakroom, Louise and David hit each other.

REMOVE THE CHILD FROM THE SITUATION

Give yourself and the children time to calm down before trying to deal with difficult situations.

For example: when children are fighting, you might separate them and then let them settle before attempting further action.

Allow each child to give their version of what happened without interruption.

Don't concentrate on who was to blame - concentrate on ensuring that it doesn't happen again.

MAKING AMENDS

This involves the child making good what they've done wrong. If a child thinks of their own way of making good their behaviour, it will probably have more effect.

For example: somebody who has thrown water around the toilets could wipe it up, or somebody who has upset someone else could make a card to say that they are sorry.

Making amends could be an important strategy when dealing with any unwanted behaviours.

REASONING

Reasoning runs through all of the strategies. Try to explain what is expected and why.

For example, if a child is teasing another, chat with them about how they would feel if they were teased or ask them how behaving badly makes them feel.

WHICH STRATEGY?

'You wouldn't hire a steam roller if you had a walnut to crack!'

When you first see something, it may be better to use a warning than time out. If the warning fails **then** consider trying something else.

In your school you might like to consider the hierarchy of strategies you would use for dealing with different, unwanted behaviours. For example:

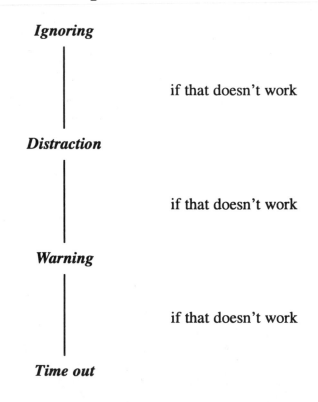

Ignoring

if that doesn't work

Distraction

if that doesn't work

Warning

if that doesn't work

Time out

POSSIBLE STRATEGIES

IGNORING

DISTRACTION

WARNINGS

REASONING

TIME OUT

REMOVE THE CHILD FROM THE SITUATION

MAKING AMENDS

CATCH GOOD BEHAVIOUR AND REWARD IT

SET RULES

CHANGE THE SETTING

AGREE SANCTIONS

SUMMARY

All children are *individual*

Behaviour difficulties are *normal*

Describe the behaviour using *non-fuzzies*

Good behaviour should be *praised*

Inappropriate behaviour should be *ignored*

Have clear *rules*

Aim for *consistency*

Match the strategy to the behaviour

LUNCH MATTERS

Session 3
Behaviour Management

Activity Materials

A LIST OF UNWANTED BEHAVIOURS

FUZZY OR NON-FUZZY?

Spot the fuzzy:
(Remember: is the verb observable and will the statement make sense if preceded by 'Hey miss, come and watch me...'?)

1. John likes a lot of attention from me.

2. Mark is always trying to get back into school to use the toilet.

3. Susan sits quietly to eat her dinner.

4. Jane is always telling tales.

5. Vanessa's home situation gives considerable cause for anxiety.

6. When at the dinner table, Peter throws food into the faces of other children.

7. June gouges the table with a knife.

8. Sharon likes to get the other children into trouble.

9. Bill is hyperactive.

10. Julie pulls hair when she cannot have a toy she wants.

11. John is always rude to me.

12. Whilst waiting in the queue for his dinner, Paul pushes the children in front of him.

CHANGE THE SETTING

Session 3: Activity C

BEHAVIOURS

Paul hurts other children

Samiha throws her food

Billy's language is dreadful

Melissa and Elizabeth often get into fights

Abdullah has temper tantrums when he doesn't want to do something

Peter has damaged a school desk

Anneka likes to tell tales on other children

John often comes into the dining hall in a bad mood. He will push in the queue, pull at other children, shout at everybody and behave badly

Alastair stuffs paper towels down the toilet

Sita is cheeky to one of the lunchtime supervisors

BEHAVIOURS

What issues about the child do you need to consider?

What issues about organisation and planning do you need to consider?

How could you change the description to be less fuzzy?

What interventions could you try?

Appendices

GENERAL PLAYGROUND ISSUES

Is there a school policy concerning playtimes and lunchtimes?

What are the playground rules?

Is playtime included in the curriculum?

Do children know how to play?

How are policies on racism and sexism applied in the playground?

Are supervisory staff aware of Health and Safety Issues and First Aid?

THE STATUS OF LUNCHTIME SUPERVISORS

Are the supervisors part of the school community, eg included in the school handbook, introduced in assembly, invited to social events, receive school letters?

Do supervisors take part in discussions about policies relating to lunchtimes?

Do supervisors have opportunities to attend training courses?

Do supervisors have a range of sanctions and rewards which they can use?

Is there a place allocated to supervisors to meet and store their belongings?

ORGANISATION

Are there opportunities for supervisors to meet with the headteacher or other teaching staff?

Is there a 'handing over' time between supervisors and teaching staff at the start of and/or the end of lunchtime?

How are supervisors informed of the special needs or individual circumstances of children?

Are there opportunities for supervisors to work with a particular group of children in order to establish relationships?

What equipment is available to support both indoor and outdoor play?

LUNCH MATTERS

AGENDA

SESSION 1

9.15 - 9.30	Arrival and Registration
9.30 - 10.30	The Role of the Lunchtime Supervisor and the Personal Qualities/Skills Needed to do the job
10.30 - 10.45	Tea/Coffee and Biscuits
10.45 - 11.30	Organising for a Better Lunchtime

* * * * *

SESSION 2

9.15 - 9.30	Arrival and Registration
9.30 - 10.30	Understanding Play
10.30 - 10.45	Tea/Coffee and Biscuits
10.45 - 11.30	Developing Play

* * * * *

SESSION 3

9.15 - 9.30	Arrival and Registration
9.30 - 10.30	Strategies for Behaviour Management
10.30 - 10.45	Tea/Coffee and Biscuits
10.45 - 11.30	More Strategies for Behaviour Management

LUNCH MATTERS!

This is to Certify

that

_____

has attended a course of training
for lunchtime supervisors.

The course covered:

- the role of the lunchtime supervisor
- the importance of play
- ideas for developing play
- behaviour management strategies

Signature _____ Date_____

References and Further Reading

Blatchford, P. and Sharp, S. (1994) (eds) *Breaktime and the School: Understanding and Changing Playground Behaviour,* London: Routledge.

Blatchford, P. (1989) *Playtime in the Primary School: Problems and Improvements,* Windsor: NFER-Nelson.

Blatchford, P. (1998) *Social Life in School: Pupils' Experience of Breaktime and Recess from Seven to Sixteen Years,* London: The Falmer Press.

Christie, J. F. (1991) *Play and Early Years Development,* Albany, New York: State University of New York Press.

Department for Education and Science (DES) (Elton Report) (1989) *Discipline in Schools: Report of the Committee of Enquiry,* Chaired by Lord Elton, London: HMSO.

Grudgeon, E. (1993) 'Gender implications of playground culture', in Woods, P. and Hammersley, M. (eds) *Gender and Ethnicity in Schools: Ethnographic Accounts,* London: Routledge.

Hillman, M. (1993) 'One False Move...' in Hillman, M. (ed) *Children, Transport and the Quality of Life,* London: Policy Studies Institute.

Karklins, J. and Kirby, P. (1993) *Midday Supervision: An In-Service Training Programme,* Norwich: Norfolk Educational Press.

Keaney, B. and Lucan, B. (1993) (eds) *Bright Ideas: The Outdoor Classroom,* Scholastic Publications Ltd.

Kelly, E. (1988) 'Pupils, racial groups and behaviour in schools', in Kelly, E. and Cohn, T., *Racism in Schools: New Research Evidence,* Stoke-on-Trent: Trentham.

Kelly, E. (1994) 'Racism and sexism in the playground', in Blatchford, P. and Sharp, S. (eds) *Breaktime and the School: Understanding and Changing Playground Behaviour,* London: Routledge.

Leeds Integrated Support Service, *Organisation and Management of Lunchtimes: A Course for Lunchtime Supervisors and Supervisory Assistants,* Leeds: Leeds City Council Department of Education.

Mooney, A., Creeser, R. and Blatchford, P. (1991) 'Children's views on teasing and fighting in junior schools', *Educational Research,* 33, 2, pp.103-112.

Mosley, J., *Create Happier Lunchtimes: Ideas for Primary Midday Supervisors,* Wiltshire: Wiltshire Education Support and Training.

Mosley, J. (1991) *Guidelines for Primary Midday Supervisory Assistants,* Wiltshire: Wiltshire Education Support and Training.

Moyles, J. R. (1988) (ed) *The Excellence of Play,* Buckingham: Open University Press.

Newcastle Upon Tyne Education Authority (1990) *Midday Supervision Training Package,* Newcastle: Newcastle Education Authority.

Opie, I. and Opie, P. (1969) *Children's Games in Street and Playground*, London: Oxford University Press.

OPTIS (1986) *Lunchtime Supervision*, Oxford: Oxfordfordshire County Council Education Department.

Ross, C. and Ryan, A. (1991) *Can I Stay in Today Miss?: Improving the School Playground*, Stoke-on-Trent: Trentham Books.

Sayeed, Z. and Guerin, E. (2000) *Early Years Play: A Happy Medium for Assessment and Intervention*, London: David Fulton.

Sluckin, A. (1981) *Growing up in the Playground: The Social Development of Children*, London: Routledge and Kegan Paul.

Sutton-Smith, B. (1990) 'School playground as festival', *Children's Environments Quarterly*, 7, 2, pp.3-7.

S.T. Books, *The Wet Playtime Book*, West Sussex: S. T. Books.

Thorne, B. (1993) *Gender play: Girls and Boys in School*, Buckingham: Open University Press.

Tizard, B., Blatchford, P., Burke, J., Farquhar, C. and Plewis, I. (1988) *Young Children at School in the Inner City*, Hove: Lawrence Erlbaum Associates.

Walker, I., Mayall, L. and Gregory, D. (1993) *Training Lunchtime Organisers*, Manchester: Manchester City Council Education Department.

White, A. and Wilkinson, J. (1996) *Playtimes and Playgrounds*, Lucky Duck Publishing.

Whitney, I. and Smith, P. (1993) 'A survey of the nature and extent of bully/victim problems in junior/middle and secondary schools', Educational Press, 35, pp.3-25.